The 4 Element Cal

by

Josef Reisz

This Sales Pocket Guide is a concise, easy-to-read book that will help you get more business.

It's the only sales book that shows you how to use the 4 elements of a sales call and turn it into an opportunity to demonstrate your solution's capabilities to solve your prospect's challenges.

This book will show you how to:

1. Go into the opening of your sales call,

2. Gather intelligence from your prospects,

3. Demonstrate your solution's capabilities to solve their challenges

4. Obtain their commitment

About Josef Reisz

Josef Reisz is a CEO with over 25 years of experience in the development of new markets, strategic planning and implementation.

Josef has been on both sides of the table; as an Entrepreneur, he started out by founding six successful companies, such as VU Capital, JRC Strategic Business Advisory and, most recently, HoneyComb Agency.

He also has extensive experience working for Fortune 500 corporations as well as smaller privately-owned businesses - holding various roles such as Head of Sales, Marketing and eCommerce.

Josef Reisz is a serial entrepreneur with an impressive track record. He has had experience in various roles on the C- and Board level held positions as Head of Sales, Head of Marketing, Head of Ecommerce, CEO, Non-Exec and Advisory Board member.

Josef has written five books on topics ranging from personal growth to business success. His writings have helped countless people build better lives while growing their respective brands or companies.

About HoneyComb

HoneyComb is A Team Of Creative Strategists Who Love Crafting Beautiful, Smart And Inspired Strategies That Help Businesses Meet Their Most Ambitious Objectives.

HoneyComb provides In-Depth training with a proven track-record for sales organisations that enables them to hit their targets, stay motivated and incentivised, close more deals and generate more, predictable revenue for your organisation.

Fast-track Transformation of Organisations And Teams Into Well-Oiled, Homogenous And Inspired Powerhouses By Strategic Design.

www.HoneyCombAgency.co.uk

HONEYCOMB

Introduction

In the world of sales, a meeting can make or break your day. It is difficult to engage with someone who is unwilling to listen and it is impossible to get them on board if they don't know what you are talking about. This book will teach you how to have a successful sales call by teaching you the 4 elements that comprise one: opening, gathering intelligence, demonstrating capabilities and obtaining commitment.

Why is it important to know these four elements and how to apply them?

The world of sales is tough and getting more competitive every day. In order to stand out from the rest, you must have a good understanding of these four elements so that when it comes time for you to close the deal, there will be no doubt in your mind as to whether or not they are going to buy.

Why do we need to structure our sales calls?

Once we have a structure we can focus on our objective and our objective almost any time in any sales call is to close the deal, close the lead and turn them into a buying customer.

Once you know the structure, and memorized it, you can speak with authority and confidence, which is absolutely crucial, especially in the first 15 to 30 seconds, that really needs to be spot on one thing that you can do.

I always recommend to draft a sales script or a call guide. And use that in every call you make. All the great sales people have a sales script because it just helps them to focus.

Winging it is the worst sales practice and will not lead to outstanding results.

A great sales script based on the 4 elements of a sales call helps you to build your authority and to get through that crucial opening in the first 15 to 30 seconds.

The structure also gives us flexibility throughout the call because once we have the structure and we have the structure in front of us, we can jump back and forth to wherever we need to be in the conversation, depending on how the conversation goes, depending on what information we can gather from our prospect.

The 4 Elements of A Sales Call

Opening

The crucial first 15-30 seconds

The first 15 to 30 seconds are absolutely crucial, because that's when we need to establish our authority.

That's when we need to convince our prospect that they should listen and pay attention to what we have say.

We don't want them just immediately shutting us down or immediately saying, "No." We want to make a good, enticing first impression that piques their interest, and have them stay engaged.

Opening a sales call is where many sales people struggle and get frustrated. Once they get their decision makers on the call, they are faced with 'no time', 'no interest', or 'where did you get my number from' responses.

Hence, it is imperative to prepare each and every call specifically and diligently. Get informed about your prospect and their business. Do your research beforehand so you can show them you know what you're talking about.

Example:

"Hi Ian, This is Josef Reisz with HoneyComb. I hope you're well. I read on your website today that you are hiring 5 new sales people. Congrats on the growth! Mind if I ask you one question, if I may. From working other customers in your sector, we know that a new sales rep takes roughly 6-9 months before they're fully productive. Out of curiosity: How are you planning on giving your new hires the proper training on the job?"

Showing Authority

As we said earlier it's crucial to establish our authority. We do that by telling them why they should listen to us and pay attention to what we have say. We need to make sure that they are with us in this conversation and paying attention.

Why is it important for you to show authority in the opening of your sales call?

It is absolutely crucial because if your prospect doesn't think you have the authority they will shut down and stop listening to what we say. They won't see any value in having a conversation with you.

You can show authority by your knowledge about the prospect themselves, knowledge about their current business strategy, or other factors such as a joint venture, for example.

Authority in this case does not mean to be bullish and arrogant. Nothing could be further from that. What it means is that you have the knowledge and understanding to be able to engage them in a meaningful conversation relevant to their situation.

Speak with Confidence

You have to speak with confidence. Never be apologetic or put yourself in a lesser position, even when speaking to a C-Level executive. You are in a position to add value to their business and that should be your mindset.

Believe in yourself, and believe that you can add value to this person's business.

Why is it so important to portrait confidence within the first 30 seconds?

It is so important because if you don't believe in yourself or the value that you have to offer, then why should your prospect? They will just shut down. You need to speak with confidence and knowledge of this person's business before they even begin to trust your words.

What do you need to get done before the call to have THAT confidence? You should always be prepared and look over your notes. If you are not familiar with what they have gone through, it is good practice to read their website or blog which can give insight on how they run their business and where they may want to expand in the future.

How can you build up your confidence levels right before your sales call?

It is important to take a few deep breaths and visualize yourself succeeding in the call. If you are not prepared, it can be helpful to go over your notes one more time before heading into your sales meeting.

What does confidence do? Why is that so important? Confidence makes people feel comfortable speaking with you about their business . If you don't display a confident attitude, your prospect will not be open to speaking with you about their business or what they are looking for.

What is the biggest mistake most sales people make when trying to build confidence?

The biggest mistake that some salespeople make in building up their confidence is thinking too much before making the call. It can be helpful to walk around the office and take a few deep breaths, but you do not want too much time passing. If it is your first call of the day (which I recommend), then get in there!

One final piece of advice on building confidence for salespeople?   One last piece of advice that can help build   confidence is to practice your pitch in front of a mirror or in a role play with colleagues or line managers. This can be helpful because you will know exactly what words are coming out of your mouth, and it becomes more natural for you.

Introduce yourself

The first rule: Keep this short and sweet.

The call is not about you or your product and services. It is, in fact, irrelevant.

Introduce yourself. *"This is MY NAME from YOUR COMPANY."*

What you can do to get straight in the conversation is to ask a simple question:

"Have you heard of us?"

If your prospect replies with 'Yes', your next best move is to ask them further *"Great! What exactly have you heard of us?"*

Another example:

[Prospect's first name], YOUR NAME calling from YOUR COMPANY. I hope you're well. The reason for my call...[refer to a previous conversation with

the prospect or their business, or an internal / external Trigger Event - and then lead into the conversation]

Recap previous conversations

Recapping previous conversations in your sales call is a great way to get into the conversation. In this case, it does not matter if you had the conversation with your prospect or one of their colleagues. You might even use a conversation one of your own colleagues had in the past with the target company and refer to that.

When you recap previous conversations with your prospect you ensure that both of you are on the same page immediately. Chances are they might not remember everything that was said in the previous call. Therefore, it is helpful to make notes and put your notes into your CRM system where you can always access it right in time for your next call.

Remember: If they don't remember what was said in a previous conversation – they are likely to be impressed with your attention to detail. Again, this shows authority and confidence. It opens the door to further questions, and it builds a strong foundation for your next conversation and moving on to the next level.

Get commitment to ask questions

Once you have that commitment, you can get the conversation flowing and lead the conversation as well. But we need that commitment and the permission so that we can ask the questions.

Here's a smart way of getting around a 'No' if you ask for permission:

'Could I ask you a question, if I may. (Tonality goes down at the end. Notice that it is NOT really a question but rather a statement, and then you go straight into your first question)

Gathering Intelligence

Every sales call is based on a set of questions that are phrase in such a way that it will enable the sales rep to gather as much intelligence about the prospect and their business as possible.

It is important to never appear to sales-y or pushy, or even desperate. You have to phrase the questions in a way that the prospect is receptive to it and opens up naturally. The more rapport you build throughout the conversation, the more likely it is that they open up and give you the information you need in order to qualify the prospect.

Regardless of the sales methodology you apply - SPIN, BANT or HoneyComb's own Sales Methodology - you should focus on asking open questions. Avoid those closed questions where the prospect has the chance to answer with just one word or one sentence. This will interrupt the conversation flow that you need and work hard to accomplish.

.

You have to control that conversation and you have to ask your questions in such a way that you get the information you need, the answers you want, and makes the prospect feel comfortable to open up.

Examples of questions you should prepare in advance in a well-drafted sales script"

- Situational Questions
- Challenges Questions
- Impact Questions
- Gap Questions
- Authority / Budget Questions

This is where the art of sales comes in. You need to phrase every question in such a way to the answer will lead to the outcome that you want. Hence, it is crucially important that you know your Value Proposition inside out, the benefits and advantages of your solution and have a good insight into your prospect's mindset and their business.

This is where you have to fill in the gap between their current situation, their objectives for the next 12-18 months, and where your solutions fits in to bridge the gap between 'Current Situation' and 'Future Ideal'.

You want to have meaningful conversations with our prospects and these conversations need to be customer-centric. The sales and buyer landscape has drastically changed with the advent of social media. Power has shifted from the Seller-side to the Buyer-side.

Buyers are much more sophisticated, and have better access to more relevant information than ever before.

That's why it's very important to have a sales script. Know the structure of a sales call and the important elements of the sales call, so you can always revert back to that, and you are always focused and confident.

Situation

What is the current state of affairs, aka situation with your prospect and in their business? Asking questions about their situation in relation to the solution you are offering are crucial to understand where your value proposition can come in to add value to their bottom-line.

What are your prospect's business drivers to facilitate a decision to engage with a third-party provider?

What are the major pain points your prospects are experiencing with their current solution? What does success look like for them and what is not working out as expected to date?

Business drivers are a great way of identifying what your prospect would add as a deciding factor when making a decision. Is it revenue, cash flow, cutting costs, increase team productivity, minimise onboarding time for new hires? It can be anything related to your value proposition.

Some of these factors, you can easily research before making the call. By doing so, you are prepared and you can show your prospect that you are knowledgable about their business, demonstrate authority and expertise.

Business Objectives

What are the business objectives for the next 12-18 months, and what is your prospected company's timeframe for implementing these changes? Ask questions about their goals, challenges they might be facing and how your solution can help them achieve these in a smart way.

Gathering intelligence about their business goals and objectives put you in a position to highlight your solution's added value and ways of utilising your product or services in order to achieve your prospect's goals faster, easier, cheaper, more efficiently, etc.

How long have they been trying to accomplish these things? And why hasn't it worked so far? What were the challenges they were facing along their journey?

Notice that you can jump between situation, challenges, impact questions throughout your sales conversation. This is not a rigid template to follow. It is a framework that will help you to keep the conversation flowing, meaningful and customer-centred.

Gap

Where does your prospect see themselves within this year to 18 months - where do they want to stand - and where are they now?

Asking questions to identify the gap between 'Current Situation' vs their 'Future Ideal', will enable you to create a meaningful conversation with your prospect and to understand where your solution potentially can fit into their picture.

What are the primary things that need to be addressed immediately in order for your prospect's business, team or organisation, to begin moving towards their 'Future Ideal'?

You will notice that some of these questions can overlap. That is because it really depends on what you know about your prospect's situation - if they have been having a difficult time with certain aspects of their business, then it might be a good idea to focus on those first.

These questions help you understand what solution/approach and how much value your prospect expects from engaging with you or your product/service.

Developing rapport, trust and credibility with your prospect is crucial for a successful sales conversation - you can do so by asking open-ended questions that don't have one or two word answers.

You want to get under the surface and understand what makes your prospects tick. Even if they are not going to be buying from you, you can still learn a lot by asking the right questions and paying attention to their answers.

You will find that some of these questions might not apply at all given your prospect's situation - so feel free to skip them or modify/customise as per your needs and preferences.

Challenges

What challenges are your prospect's business currently facing? How are they going about it now? What did work, what did not?

By asking well-formulated, prepared questions about their challenges, you will be able to bring out their pain points without explicitly saying it yourself.

Craft your questions in such a way that they are non-intrusive and gives the prospect the freedom to give you all the answer you need - and want - to direct the conversation to the solutions you provide and the value you can add to your prospect's business.

You want to ask your prospects questions in such a way so that you can understand what their current challenges are. In relation to your solution, it is crucial for you to draft a strong value proposition because by doing so you will already have an understanding of some of the challenges your target accounts are facing.

Draft a strong sales script and call guide with relevant questions and formulate the questions in such a way that the outcome, i.e. your prospect's response, will dip into your value proposition.

Be prepared to ask questions that will give you value-add insights, which in turn can help create a more targeted proposition for your prospect's business.

It is important that before any sales call or appointment, be it a discovery call , qualification call or demo/presentation opportunity - always carry out research on the account beforehand and gather as many insights as possible.

Typically, business challenges can be found on the company's website, press releases, LinkedIn and so fourth. Do your research and adapt your script accordingly.

Always make sure that the questions you ask are not intrusive and do not come across as a sales pitch.

When asked in appropriate situations, prospect's will be more than happy to share their challenges with you, especially when it is presented in such a way where they can give insight into how they currently deal with this challenge.

Present yourself as a consultant rather than a sales person. Being a consultant automatically puts you in a better position because you can detach from the outcome, yet add value to your prospect during your conversation.

Impact

What is the impact of these challenges on their business, employees and bottom-line? What does it cost your prospect to remain the status quo with all their current challenges?

Craft your questions in such a way that you are able to bring out the financial impact of these challenges.

Ask questions about what would be the positive outcome if they overcame this challenge or how much money it costs them every year in terms of revenue loss.

By asking well-formulated questions with a desired outcome in mind you will know when to start discussing possible solutions. Preferably yours.

The current situation, challenge, impact, financial cost and solution - This is what you need to know before going into any further sales conversation with your prospect. Your questions should be well thought-out so that they will go along with your pitch for why they should choose you as their potential partner instead of continuing on without a solution.

Your prospect will be looking for a confident partner that they can trust and rely on to provide results, so make sure you highlight your expertise in this particular space, i.e. Demonstrating Capabilities, as well as what makes it easier for them by having you work with them instead of just another company who is not specialized in their industry or isn't able to give them the personal attention they require.

Authority / Budget

Are there any key decision makers or influencers involved in this sales cycle?

What is the budget for making a purchase - what does it take and how important is it for them to solve their problems right now, next month or next year?

Authority and budget are closely linked as they both depend on each other for the final decision to be made.

It is important that you know who all the key players in this particular sale are, what their roles are and how much influence they will have over a purchase decision.

Having this knowledge about your prospects makes it easier for you to plan and execute your sales strategy.

Make sure that you also include the budget in your questioning so that it is clear how much money they have (or are able to) set aside for this particular purchase.

This information will be helpful when developing a pitch as well as presenting any offers or pricing regarding your product or service.

Should you be targeting big accounts, ask a simple question, such as:

"Would such a project fall into this year's or next year's budget?"

"How do you usually sign off on a project like this?"

Demonstrating Capabilities

You are now at a point in your conversation where you can and must demonstrate your capabilities of solving your prospect's challenges and solving their problems.

Stick to the order of the 4 elements of your sales call. Here's the reason why:

If you mention your capabilities earlier in the conversation, that can be perceived as pushy or sales-y. Stick to the four elements in the order outlined in this book.

At that point, you have the permission to explain what you do, to explain what you do, and how it would benefit your prospects.

By asking our questions in a strategic and customer centric way, you understand what potential benefits they are looking for in a solution, their future objectives, the current situation, their pain points and gaps, their challenges, the implications of remaining with the status quo, and so forth. This position allows us now to understand what benefits your prospects are looking for. And the best part? It's coming out of their mouth, not yours.

Your Value Proposition

In order to demonstrate capabilities, it is extremely helpful to have a strong value proposition at hand which is tailored to your prospect's industry or sector and covers business drivers, movement and metrics.

It is absolutely essential that you are able to use this part of your sales call to demonstrate how your solution has helped other businesses similar to your prospect, what it did for them and how they benefitted from your solution.

Power Statement

Start with a simple Power Statement, such as:

We help sales teams break into big accounts, get c-level decision makers on the phone and close them faster than before.

Then, you can bring in a recent example, such as:

In every sales team we speak to today, new customer acquisition is crucial. Their pipelines might be filled but they're having a hard time getting prospects on the phone, getting replies to their emails and closing them.

Recently we did a project with a large company in the education space. The business had been stale for 5 years with no growth.

We worked with them to develop strategies to get recurring revenue from existing customers that hadn't been contacted for years and winning new clients with specific outreach campaigns.

Results? 61% uplift in revenue within 3 months.

So tell me: How is your sales team doing with your existing pipeline and new customer acquisition? Is it more challenging now than before?

Your Value Proposition needs to consist of:

1. Business Driver (e.g. Revenue or cost savings)

2. Movement (increase, decrease)

3. Metrics (X%)

Followed immediately by a proven example / track record as in the example above.

In a nutshell:

- Talk about your solution only after the prospect has explained their pain-points, situation and implication to you.

- By asking our questions in a strategic, customer-centric way, you understand what benefits they are looking for in a solution.

- If you then can demonstrate your capabilities of solving their problems and adding benefits that is the moment to obtain your prospect's commitment to the next step.

Forget about Features

It is of utmost importance not to talk about features and technicalities, but rather the benefits to your prospect and their bottom-line.

If you are a product-focused company that wants to sell your products or services based on their own merits, then this step should be easier for you than if it's your company speciality - which might be when you have more complex solutions with several technical features and capabilities.

When you show your prospect the benefits of what it will do for them, then they should naturally be inclined to buy from you without having to sell too hard or pushy. You have demonstrated that this is a win-win situation for both parties involved (Seller and Buyer).

Obtaining Commitment

Obtaining commitment from your prospect in your sales call is an imperative step to move on in your sales funnel and keep your prospect 'in line' with your objectives.

The closing part of the sales call is the fourth stage in your cold call.

What's your Next Step?

It can be anything from:

• A Lead Handover for a demonstration

• A Future Call Back

• Send more Information

• A Proposal

• Have them schedule an appointment

Whatever it might be, make sure you know what it is - don't laugh, some sales reps have no clue what their next step is - , and that you and your prospect are on the same page.

The Psychology behind it

Psychologically, getting someone's commitment makes it hard for them to break their promise once it's given. This is a huge advantage for you as the sales person, because once you get your prospect to commit, they are more likely to follow through with what has been agreed upon.

The thing is: In order for someone's commitment to be of any value, it must be given sincerely and voluntarily when the person in question was not under pressure or duress from anyone else; otherwise it might just as well have never happened, which is a shame in such an important part of the sales process.

Never force obtaining commitment

The other thing you have to keep in mind when obtaining commitment from your prospect during your call is that they should not feel 'backed into' any sort of corner or forced somehow; this will only make them react defensively and close up on you instead of being forthcoming with what they really think and feel, which is of course the opposite effect you are after.

What's more: if your prospect feels forced into taking one action or another it will make them resentful - a very powerful negative emotion that can lead to all sorts of bad behaviour in both business and personal life.

So don't force anyone into anything.

Conclusion

By now, you have seen the four elements of a sales call. Before picking up the phone and making that next call, make sure that you have clarified your next step and what it is going to be.

If you can obtain commitment from a prospect before the close of your sales call, then you are well on your way for closing deals faster than ever!

Remember: Don't talk features or technicalities until they've explained their situation to you in detail.

Define your sales process and make sure that you follow it.

Make an effort in mapping out the different elements of a successful Sales Call with your prospect, so everyone is on board and knows exactly what they are doing next.

This will lead to more clarity, more commitment at every step of the way - which leads to higher closing rate.

Printed in Great Britain
by Amazon

65959319R00031